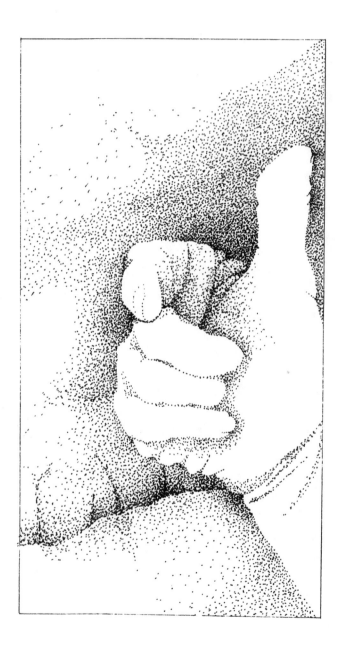

mary howes

lying in bed

with drawings by jane ross

Longspoon Press

ISBN 0-919285-06-6

Edited for the Press by Douglas Barbour

Typesetting and layout: Marni L. Stanley

THE LONGSPOON PRESS
c/o Dept. of English
University of Alberta
Edmonton, Alberta
T6G 2E5

Longspoon Press is a mail order press.
Books should be ordered directly from the publisher.

Longspoon Press wishes gratefully to acknowledge financial
assistance for the publication of *Lying in Bed* from
THE EMIL SKARIN FUND, University of Alberta

The only people for me are the mad ones.
The ones who are mad to live, mad to talk,
mad to be saved, desirous of everything
at the same time, the ones who never yawn or say
a commonplace thing but burn, burn, burn
like fabulous yellow roman candles exploding
like spiders across the stars.

-*Kerouac*

Bless me father, for I have sinned. I committed
endoarchy two times, melanicity four times,
encropatomy seven times, and prepocity with
igneous intent, pretolemicity and overt cranial-
ism once each.

-*Barthelme*

i'd like to say hello to bob howes

if he's out there watching

the title poem

lying

in

bed

is

easier

than

telling

the

truth

standing

up

assumed identity

i could have been someone else
the one you met
somewhere else
the one you dream of

you can't be sure
even now
although i am so familiar to you

still
i am no one you know
so it could have been me
you can't be sure

martini sex

i like my women
straight up
with a twist

too bad
i like my men
on the rocks

marine life

woman at the sink
moving her mouth
lip sync
eye swim
tearing greens
to pieces
no sound
but the water
rushing
down the drain
endlessly
making salads
with her hands
turning red
underwater
drowning in greens
shaking oil and lemon
shaking salt and pepper
tossing everything
up for grabs
turning from the sink
treading water
she serves supper on time
as usual

what he left me for

lapis lazuli eyes

and

wild wine lips

a regular
nature girl

she
spends
her
time

extracting
essences
from

rocks

and

berries

who says you can't squeeze blood from a stone

living in cold countries

three swedish icicles
dripping in the doorway
almost grim isn't it

the way these sisters wring
their pale ringed hands
powerless in the hands of the master

greed
pain
perversity

they eat them for dinner
on white damask
and the red walls behind them

bleed into their faces
one by one   they interpret
ecstasy through the master's eye

maria heaves her ample bosom
cut low for exposure
and dreams of standing still

as she always does
watching her husband stick a knife
in his gut and beg for help

karin clutches at her throat
in its high black collar
and remembers the night

she got even with her body
for just being there   attached to her
such a brilliant piece of cinema

to watch a woman lacerate her cunt
with a broken wineglass
then open her legs to her husband

she can't resist dipping a hand in
smearing blood over her lips
little deaths are few and far between

agnes is a simpler sort
having nothing much to clutch or heave
she contents herself with

dying
a slow   horrible   painful   death
right there in front of everyone

she convulses   vomits   beats a tattoo
on her wasted chest
she smiles like a saint

anna the maidservant
lost a child before the film began
has nothing else to lose

so she prepares a feast
on the altarbed
resplendent for this occasion

with fine white linens   crimson canopies
she bares her milky breast
to the aged baby cradled there

maria and karin watch this tableau
from the doorway
exposing and covering their respective breasts

they vow to become closer
in the future but for the time being
they manage to stay the same

both refuse to engage
in any communion
with the dead

oh mr. bergman
you make morbid movies
i am sick to death
of your women
whose suffering serves no purpose

i don't mind being a victim
as long as there's a reason
but you would have me believe

that being a woman
is reason enough

water dream

i dive into a still brown autumn pond
beneath me
a pale black shadow
keeps gigantic pace
as fast as i flail
i never quite reach shore
it never quite devours me

six of one

these are the thighs that drive men wild
or so i've been told
most recently by you

only hours ago poised above me
you said how familiar
my body felt to you

that soon we'd be unable to tell
where one of us left off
the other began

now
at dawn i roll over to watch
you rising to meet yourself

stroke for stroke
i'd say you met your match
long before i came on the scene

neighbourly gossip

she bathed in the dark
a candle on the tub's edge
he thought the house was empty
only wanted the tv   some silver
until he saw the flickering
heard small splashes   humming
he had to go in there
it was too tempting not to
almost justified
wouldn't you say
bathing in the dark like that
when you're home all alone

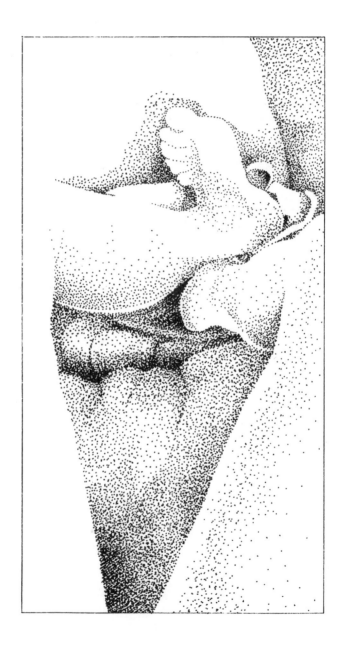

rites

one night she decided to fight him off
pummelled his shoulders with her fists
tied her legs in knots
whipped her head back and forth
screaming

he laughed at her fists
undid her legs
sucked on the strands of her hair
set her on top of him
like a toy
pulled at her nipples
slid something into her

she denied all feeling
ground her teeth to dust
willed internal tides
to ebb and die

jesus you're beautiful when you're horny he said

there's a catch to this

i don't know where to put my hands
without tipping the scales
in somebody's favour

boneless
i swim away
practise drownproofing
until the worm has turned

beached
on wet sheets
i sleep with my eyes wide open

the lure is gone but
the malady lingers on

the canadian way

i spend all my nights
trying to get away from you
in attics and cellars
dark places and damp

i push you off a cliff
i hold you underwater
i feed you poison
i slit your throat

every morning i find you
here beside me
sleeping like a newborn
it's so discouraging

i am exhausted
by these ineffectual exercises
it's time to start training
to beat you at your own game

i spend the rest of the day
in the garage
sharpening your old hockey stick
for tonight's rendezvous

electra dream

i fly through the upstairs window
land beside my father on the bed
i thought you lived in edmonton   he says
i came for a visit dad   where's mom
i follow him downstairs
in the dining room   against the sideboard
bulging   sticky   open
she's in the bags   he says
the dog comes in to sniff
i shoo him out scolding
that's all we need dad
for the neighbours to see him
chewing on her bones

my father slumps in a chair by the window
yellow roses in his lap
have you called the police
i was too tired   he says
i pick up the phone and try to dial
i try and try but i can't do it
my father snips stems
arranges roses in a vase
i sit down to watch
he is so good with flowers

connections I

when i was a girl
my mother woke up
screaming
dreaming of hotels again
secret passages
rats in the cellar
a hypnotist
hanging from a lightcord
grandpa was a hotelkeeper
and he drank too much
beat them all
locked them in closets
all her brothers and sisters
screamed too
in her dreams

me in the next room
kneeling at the window
nose against the screen
watching a summer storm
japanese maples on the boulevard
thickleafed and shining bloody
under the streetlamp
clotted gutters and manholes
gurgling
maybe a running shoe
or a trike left out
dripping

over my bed
jesus holds his bleeding heart
maria goretti virgin martyr
glows green on the dresser
a glass circle in her throat
with a scrap of the dress
she wore that day
somewhere in the house
my brothers whisper the rosary

i stay at the window
gulping
soft wet air
my mother
in the next room
screaming
when i was a girl

connections II

we sat on the porch
shelling peas
that morning
you wore a checkered apron

my bare feet swung back and forth
over the slick enamel floor
plop
plop
the peas made a pyramid in your lap
i laid my head there
and you told me something

what's important is just getting through it all
you will
i am
my mother did
and her mother too

knowing you were all there
perched above me in the family tree
was little consolation
grinning and bearing it
has never been my long suit

so i jumped down and planted my own tree
when she asks
i tell my daughter i have no idea
what's important
some advice she says
is that what grandma told you

not really she didn't have much time to chat
she was so busy getting through it all

connections III

at the swimming pool
that 14th summer
a thousand sunstars
shimmered on the water

i shimmied up over the side
shivering
drymouthed
sat on a white bench
beside the lifeguard

if you lick the water off your lips
like that one more time
he said
i'm going to go crazy
and reached over
to run his thumb
along my cheekbone

nothing
makes me
shiver
quite
like
a thumb
along my cheekbone

just thinking about it
i automatically lick my lips

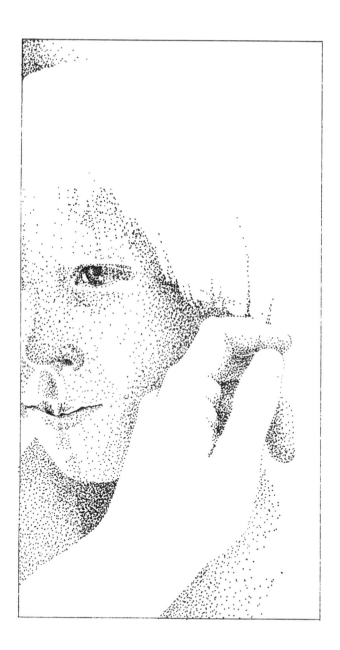

seeing my brother again

riding with dan
in his company car
top's down tonight
and he's driving like he did
when he was a kid
fast and slick with
a small grim smile

i'm content on my side
arm out the window
clicking the side view mirror around
listening to the beach boys
little deuce coupe

we're making the rounds
of pubs around kitchener
humming over the back roads
he knows so well
his territory all these years

do you remember when we were kids
how you used to cry in bed
when i sang danny boy to you
i call above the wind and the music

he wheels into a parking lot
spitting gravel
kills the motor
neon glints off his aviator glasses

c'mon sport   he says
time for sauerkraut and pigtails and beer

looney tunes

i am the woman
who lives in a basket
though my heart's not in it
i'd leave in a minute
so play us a song
and i'll come out
in a thong of rippling scales
and ascend to heights
never dreamed of before
in reptilian folklore

i've never been one
to hide my plight
under a bushel
but lately it seems
there are schemes underfoot
and lids to be put
on everything i try

i've scrambled my eggs
in different baskets around
a blue one here
green over there
and under the chair
a pink one that begs
to be cracked wide open
but i fear that my batch
whenever they hatch
will be kept in the dark
just as i've been

being locked in a basket
is taking its toll
the longer we loll undercover
it's hard to discover the light
so play us a song
and we'll perform
for the throng
and don't be alarmed dear
it's a thrill to be charmed dear
i'm sure by the pure clear
notes of your flute
not to mention the ultimate
intention is to make us stay
there in mid-air without any strings
ahhh   such a mystical thing
at this time   in this place
to finally release a basket case

the portrait speaks

my face cannot contain everything
you want to say about me   who am i
do you remember how you blurred me
at the edges   trapped under glass
you hung me smiling there in front of you
watch me watching you pace back and forth
whatever borders you had in mind
i bleed beyond   metamorphosed back
into a blueblack palette stain   watch me
leak through layers blotting out your first
intention to hold me there   trapped under glass
you thought you could always find me smiling
one eye blued   hair like a raven's wing
my face cannot contain everything

little red hen

this is the story of a woman who had everything
even a walk-in closet
one day she walked into it
and didn't come out

mommy mommy come out come out said her children
she must be premenstrual said her husband
maybe she can't decide what to wear said her mother

what nobody knew was that inside the closet
there was a secret door
which when pressed in just the right spot
swung open to reveal
another closet
just my luck said the woman
i finally take the big step and get stuck
in a closet in a closet
she looked around for more doors but
there weren't any so she came out

mommy mommy you're back you're back said her children
thank god you've come to your senses said her husband
i see you haven't changed said her mother

not enough time said the woman briskly
the lasagne's ready to come out of the oven
time for dinner everyone

on the way to the kitchen the woman thought
i'll never do that again
what's the point of coming out of the closet
if everyone recognizes you
i'll have to think of another plan
and she did

20 years later

he said
what's the matter with you

i'm board
she said
feel me

he felt her
yep you're board alright
when did that happen

quite a while ago
she said
rubbing oil all over herself

well what can i do to help
he said

not much really
she said
turning out the light
but thanks for asking

well i've always tried to be aware
of any changes in you
he said
and soon began to snore

she got out of bed
went out to the balcony
and threw herself off

naturally
being board
she just cracked

and with a bit of
crazy glue
she was soon as good as before

oh well
she said
back to the old drawing board

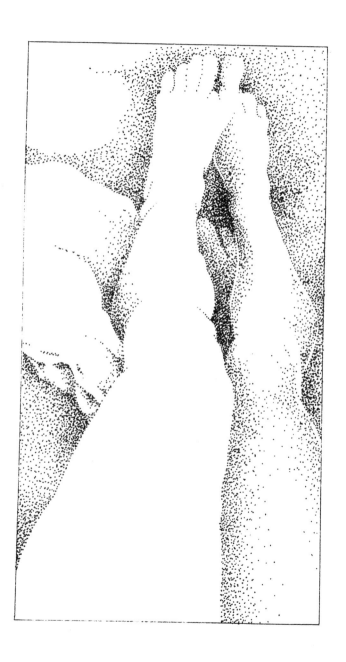

what the experts say

the opposite of love
is not hatred
it's apathy
according to rollo may
roll me over
in the clover
roll me over
lay me down
and do it again
hey hey whaddya say
about your ex-husband
you mean that
amorphous
asshole
spineless
fuckfaced
numbskull
shithead
polyester prick
see
that's not hatred
that's apathy

something electric between us

we can't go back
we go back

to an earlier time
when it was
so easy
to roll
towards each other
in the dark

magnetic fields

i love you
i love you back
and forth

sparks

we go back
we can't go back

easier now
to roll
the other way
past each other
with the punches
over
and
over
and
over

it's only static on the sheets

neon clues

i should have known
what was in store
for me
that night
in princeton

he took me
to the
ho hum motel

right across the street
from

the mediocre foodmart
the blah boutique
the passable pet store
the so so deli
the inane emporium
the pedestrian fish market
                          and
the half baked cafe

i left for the coast
in the morning
with a new respect
for
signs

neon clues
are the brightest

and they buzz
too

overheard in the antique shop

i was watching jim perry last night
we don't have cable so i gotta make do
with the canadian channels
he was talking to marj atwood
ever hear of her
well she's a real writer that one
she told him she writes 10 12 14 hours a day
and she's got a little kid too you know
seems kinda old to have a kid that age
must be a late bloomer

i slink out the back door
holy shit
marj atwood writes 10 12 14 hours a day
what the hell am i doing looking at
carnival glass in the middle of the day

what i'm good at:

meatloaf
patching jeans
christmas cookies
setting a table
setting you up
macrame plant hangers
hanging on
making ends meet
making amends
hiding the grey
hiding feelings
feeling my way
watering ferns
watering the scotch
unscrewing a jam jar
jamming the works
writing thank you notes
cutting out recipes
cutting corners
cutting you off
hospital corners
airing out quilts
piling on guilt
getting out slivers
slivering almonds
making lists
listing your faults
faultless manners
hairline fractures
fracturing an audience
auditing the books
bookbinding
binding wounds

wounding egos
rolling my own
owning up to it
uppity behaviour
behaving abominably
abdominal cramps
cramping your style
styling my hair
heretical outbursts
bursting bubbles
bubbling over
overreacting
acting the part
parting the waves
waving a white flag
flagging a cab
cabbage rolls
rolling with a punch
punch and judy shows
show and tell
telepathy
pathological lying
meatloaf

how can i keep my mouth shut at a time like this

is it time ? do you want to ? will it hurt ?
can i watch ? should i stay ? when's it on ?

what's the problem ? are you full ? is this the place ?
how's it feel ? can you taste it ? how long is it ?

was it good ? where you going ? what do you need ?
is it hard yet ? when's it over ? what's next ?

can i touch it ? will it bite ? does it tickle ?
will you wait ? can you see it ? what's your hurry ?
will i like it ? are you bored ? do you care ?
can you hear me ? did you miss it ? what about it ?

is this right ? why can't you ? since when ?
what's the prize ? do you like this ?

when's the next one ? can you slow down ?
where'd you leave it ? does it wiggle ?

are you in there ? what do i care ? why'd you stop ?
can you call back ? is it locked ? who'd you tell ?

why didn't you say something ? is this it ?
can you move it ? who said that ?

really ?
which one ?
will you ?
why not ?

is that all there is ? can't you say it ?
will you hold on a minute ? where's the exit ?

did you spill it ? what's the difference ?
how can i tell ? did i miss it ?

do you want some ? are you serious ? can you fix it ?
what's wrong with that ? where was i ?

are you coming ? what was that ? how'd that happen ?
did you say something ? what did i do ?

what's going on ? can i come in ? what's the record ?
is it open ? how long will it take ?

will you start over ? in what way ? how would i know ?
did i miss something ? what do you want ?

what do i get ? should i help myself ?
will it explode ? is that the end of it ?

who could tell ?
what's the use ?

should we ?
can i ?
does it ?
what's wrong ?
come again ?

where are you ? can i have some ? what's up ?
is it bad ? what's that smell ? who did it ?

is that the last one ? where'd you put it ?
will you stop it ? did you forget ?

who called ? did you hear something ?
can you feel that ? will it sting ?

can you swallow ? are you laughing ?
what did you do ? what's the matter with you ?

what for ?
give up ?
won't you ?
then what ?
will it ?

is that it ? what's going on ? is it broken ?
what does that mean ? are you finished ?
who told you that ? are you crazy ?

for answers see page 51

august

the wind comes up
cabbage roses
bulge into the room

i lie on the bed
book abandoned
watch the curtains
breathe faster

in
        out
in
        out
in

petite mort

this time
instead of grey birds
lifting
suddenly
into the sky
it is a grey velvet drape
folding itself
until all surfaces
meet
folds
spiral
into one another
until all folds
become
one
fold

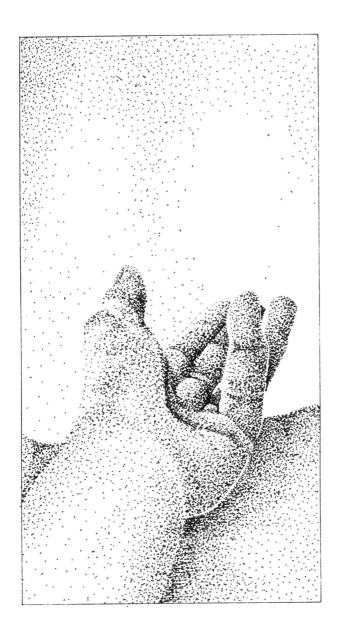

not too much to ask

i want you on top of everything else

i want you under my skin

i want you out on a limb

i want you treed

i want you floored

i want you swept under the rug

i want you in parts

i want you with one part missing

i want you reassembled

i want you behind me

i want you way in front

i want you polished

i want you varnished

i want you tarnished

i want you banished from my kingdom

i want you spinning gold

i want you on my pillow

i want you on my plate

i want you with bated breath

i want you heaving

i want you leaving

i want you believing

i want you to relieve the monotony

i want you to monopolize my time

i want you speaking in tongues

i want you tongue-tied

i want you tied up in knots

i want you climbing the castle wall

i want you tossing a golden ball

i want to carry you along

i want to let you down

i want to mess you up

i want to string you up

i want to string you a line

i want you out of sight out of mind

i want you minding the store

i want you setting your sights a little higher

i want you aiming through the cross-hairs

i want you to stop double-crossing me

i want you with my pipe and slippers

i want you with my morning kippers

i want to drag it out of you

i want you to call it off

i want you calling timber

i want you falling over

i want you standing tall

i want you here and now

i want you over there

i want you before and after

i want you sooner or later

i want you more or less

i want you better late than never

i want you tattered and torn

i want you lost and forlorn

i want you ripped to shreds

i want you mended

i want you sizzling hot

i want you fizzling out

i want you to drink me in

i want you to feast your eyes

i want you to look but don't touch

i want you to burn your fingers

i want you to thank your lucky stars

i want you in a nutshell

i want you cracked in half

i want you to spit it out

i want you to hold it in

i want you with all the wrinkles

i want you covered in warts

i want you all smoothed out

i want you gasping for breath

i want you dragging ass

i want you all fagged out

i want you gagged and bound

i want you housebound

i want you tarred and feathered

i want you to feather my nest

i want you twisting in the sheets

i want you making your own bed

i want you lying in it

i want you nodding off

i want you to step lively

i want you stepping through the looking glass

i want you tapping your toes

i want you dancing rings around me

i want you cowering in the corner

i want you towering over me

i want you in silk

i want you in lace

i want you with that look on your face

i want you to be an open book

i want you close-mouthed

i want you to expose yourself

i want you to be a pillar of salt

i want you to be the scum of the earth

i want you licking my boots

i want you to come clean

i want you hungry

i want you mean

i want you in limbo

i want you in hell

i want you to get the hell out

i want you to stay put

i want you to start talking

i want you to shut up

i want you in the back seat

i want you right up front

i want you from this moment on

i want you ticking like a bomb

i want you off in all directions

i want you to control yourself

i want you hanging from the rafters

i want you swinging on a star

i want you smoked and cured

i want you lashed to the mast

i want you walking the plank

i want you quivering on the brink

i want you up against it

i want you over the edge

i want you hook line and sinker

i want you larger than life

i want you scaled down to size

i want you in the palm of my hand

i want you under my thumb

i want to swallow you whole

i want to eat you alive

i want you begging for mercy

i want you begging for more

i want you to shoot the works

i want you to reach for the stars

i want you grasping at straws

i want you to go to the limit

i want you to pull up short

i want you hiding behind my skirts

i want you tall in the saddle

i want you riding shotgun

i want you to shoot from the hip

i want you stealing home

i want you sliding past

i want you running a red light

i want you waiting for green

i want you to piece this all together

i want you piecemeal

i want you hogtied

i want you hogwild

i want you to level with me

i want you disheveled

i want you with every hair in place

i want you to plunge in

i want you sinking to the bottom

i want you going down for the third time

i want you coming up for air

i want you slicing it close to the bone

i want you champing at the bit

i want you rising to the bait

i want you frothing

i want you first out of the shoot

i want you to chalk it up

i want you to rack it up

i want you keeping score

i want you trumping my ace

i want you calling my bluff

i want you sitting up and taking notice

i want you to open wide and take your medicine

i want you performing on a high wire

i want you wired for sound

i want you striking a balance

i want you across the finish line

i want you right across the board

i want you above board

i want you deviating from the norm

i want butter melting in your mouth

i want you over easy

i want you smelling like a rose

i want you stinking to high heaven

i want you in it up to your neck

i want you out of the picture

i want you to get the picture

i want you mastering the technique

i want you dead centre

i want you dead wrong

i want you alive and kicking

i want you rising out of the ashes

i want you to get your ashes hauled somewhere else

i want you as living proof

i want you to prove it to me

i want you to do it on your own time

i want you to get it up

i want you to let it die a natural death

i want you to let sleeping dogs lie

i want you to forgive and forget

i want you to forget we ever met

i want you to remember a worse december

i want you to put up a good front

i want you front row centre

i want you to come in out of the rain

i want you to cover yourself

i want you under my hat

i want you to try for a hat trick

i want you underfoot

i want you outside the realm of possibility

i want you tripping the light fantastic

i want to trip you up

i want you to choke it back

i want you to cough it up

i want you to leave it all behind

i want you to kiss it all goodbye

i want you to start at the beginning

i want you to start without me

i want you to end on a high note

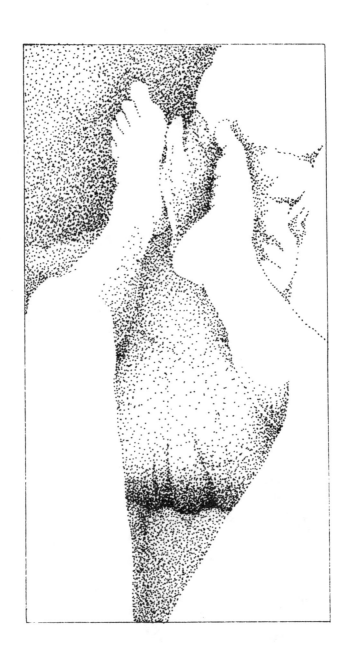

the correct answer poem

no the flight's been delayed
i'd rather play scrabble
only for a minute
if you keep your mouth shut
i want to be alone
at 9:30

it doesn't fit
i couldn't eat another bite
it feels like it
kinda stiff
there's too much curry in it
about 3 feet

dragged in the last act
out for cigarettes
crisco and a box of Q tips
you better keep pulling it
in december
charlie's angels

okay but don't drop it
no it's been spayed
only when you use a feather
if you don't take all night
it's too dark in here
i'm going to the dentist
you should   it cost enough
i'm enthralled
not really but no anchovies
i'm not deaf
just by inches
too sleazy

grab it with both hands
because i'm going to reno
1967
a plastic pig
i think it stinks

51

not for 10 years
i'm only doing 65
on the back of the toilet
no it's dead

under the bed
apathetic bitch
i have to go the the bathroom
i'm in a phone booth
i checked three times
the avon lady

i was too embarassed
close enough
we'll need 4 guys
st. matthew

yeah
the one with the limp
after the pta meeting
i'm not in the mood

there's more in the fridge
not with my mouth full
i'm losing my grip
down this aisle and turn left

only a little on the rug
2,889
you have to take the wrapper off first
it was the last cloverleaf

just a little piece
no i'm terminal
if all the parts are here
you lit the filter end
she pricks her finger on the spinning wheel

i'm just breathing hard
phil donahue
it went through the wringer
you and i babe we'll be riding high babe
you added the oil too fast

just a friendly game of poker
if you promise not to scream
the 100 in 4 flat
it's stuck again
usually 9 months

it was the best of times it was the worst of times
the american way
you've got a ph d
the part where polanski slits his nose
butterfly shrimp

satisfaction
the lord helps those
only if you light it
if there are 36 on the roll

nobody could if you leave your boots on
don't give me that crap

everything points in that direction
you can do anything
not in the light of day
my zipper's stuck
try to read my lips

in the sandbox
it'll rot your teeth
the pyramid scam collapsed
you better sit down
limburger cheese
the guy with the eyepatch

there's more in the glove compartment
under the piano
i haven't even started yet
i thought i had it right here

gloria steinem
go back to sleep   it's only coyotes
press harder
only for a minute

it hurts my throat
i'm not that morbid
tied it to a tree
the doctor says it's herpes

a dollar forty-nine
one more clue
i'll do better than that
the mice turn into horses
sometimes they need more glue

you wanted maybe a stallion
we're playing doctor
just cracked
good riddance in french
i finished 10 minutes ago
freud
not so's anybody'd notice

real myth no. 283

according to the manual
the trick to winning
a tug of war
is the amount
of tension
applied
so
at the international
women's day picnic
our side won
because we picked
only those women
who were premenstrual

real myth no. 623

lady caroline lamb's fetal body mask
use it daily
and discover
a new you
eternally

moisturized texturized revitalized whipped greaseproof
fluffy reconditioned creamy velvety delicate glossy
longlasting shimmering glowing misty luxurious satiny
concentrated seductive lustrous pearlescent and emollient

just like dewy-lynn princeton
(she knows what to wear on sunday
when she won't be home til monday)
former miss world and now
certified egyptologist and part-time naturopath

dewy-lynn speaks 7 languages and holds a cerise belt
in tai chi besides being international president
of mensa   lead soprano in the church choir and
every other weekend surrogate partner at the local
impotence and frigidity clinic

as a single parent dewy-lynn relaxes at home
cooking cordon bleu dinners for her two adorable
adopted physically handicapped racially mixed children

although dewy-lynn is a golden-ager she prides herself
on the number of wolf whistles she gets every day
jogging past construction sites

it's because i'm stacked and multi-orgasmic
admits the youthful dewy-lynn in 7 languages
i owe it all to lady caroline lamb's fetal body mask
i don't leave home without it

real myth no. 781

what's for dessert
cherries and whipped cream
great   where is it
inside me
what
i put it inside me
what
i'm just trying to spice up our sex life
jesus   you've really flipped out
it's a real treat   you'll like it
are you kidding
truman capote says there's a whorehouse in new orleans
　　　　　　very exclusive of course and every sunday
　　　　　　they serve up this dessert   that's where
　　　　　　i got the recipe
from truman capote
yeah
what the fuck does he know about whores   he's a fag
well maybe he's platonic friends with them
so what am i supposed to do about this specialty of the house
use your imagination
i think i'm going to be sick
c'mon   hurry up   i've been lying here with my legs propped up
　　　　for half an hour so i won't spill any
you really think this will help our sex life
it's worth a try
listen honey   we're ordinary people here   we live in a trailer
　　　　　　i work on the rigs   this isn't new orleans
ooohhh   poor sport   i thought you'd get a kick out of it
just clean yourself up and go out to the kitchen and heat up
　　　some of that leftover pie for me
yeah   well so much for spice
and quit reading that queer's cookbook   stick to madame benoit

real myth no. 309

tearing into lobster tails
with butter dripping lips
and snarling smiles

and then we go to bed

my legs
white pincers

hold you there

until you feel the teeth
and your worst fears come true

say uncle and i'll let you go

obedience training

you come into me from behind
good
i can't see anything this way
it could be
a wand
a bone
here rover
lie down
roll over
play dead

absolutely nothing to get alarmed about

you bitch about
the balance of power
being shifted

so i'm always on top now
and you're always
underneath

but secretly
haven't you always wanted to be a victim
                          to be forced
                          to be passive

c'mon
admit it

you love it this way

being fed at night
without a spoon

60

period piece

it's as though all your young life
you've been waiting
on tiptoe

emergency room
red blanket
emergency room
red blanket

we keep them in a hut
away from the others
or
the wine sours

squat slightly
with legs apart

waiting for a wonderful
adventure
and then one day
you make your debut

thirsty
lethargic
feverish
disoriented
blotchy
hallucinatory

iron rusts
bright mirrors dull
clocks stop

place one foot on the toilet
or on a chair

i was rolling around on the floor
screaming with pain
and my mother says
well you've got it now

no need to worry
about odour
sudden flow
revealing lines
it's absolutely impossible
for anyone to know
you've got it

we're not getting a pulse here
pressure's falling

dogs become rabid
cows abort
fruit withers and dies on the vine

sit on the toilet seat
with knees apart

don't tell your father
just come to me when it happens
and hide all that stuff
on the bottom shelf

joanie joanie
she's riding the cotton pony

feeling upset at this time
is just giving in
smart girls don't give in to
cramps
nausea
vomiting
headaches
dizziness
diarrhea
flushes
backache
fainting

keep out of drafts
don't wash your hair
showers only   no baths

affected organs:
kidney
liver
pancreas
stomach
heart
brain
and the skin peels off
like potato chips

light
discreet
effective
protection

oh for god's sake
quit carrying on like that
it's only a few days a month

auntie rose has come to visit

look at this
we were just moving her onto the stretcher
and her hair came out in clumps

clean and easy
even for beginners
your fingers never touch it
or the vaginal opening

ooo
ooo
what a smell
sally's got her period
and we can tell

i don't know what to do about all you women
here's a prescription
try to keep busy   carry on normally

look at this mess
didn't you know it was coming
change those sheets quick
before your brother comes in

she's on the kidney machine
respirator
heart monitor
the works

the key to easy and proper
insertion
is to relax and take your time

what do you mean you don't want to
are you on the rag again
i swear you've got it every other week

so comfortable
you may forget it's in there

i told you to take the cardboard off
before you put it in
no wonder you can hardly walk

intensive care
code 7
intensive care
code 7

it's a sign from god
you're a woman now

for an added touch
of freshness
now deodorized

what's that on the back of your skirt

should there be any discomfort
it has not been inserted deeply enough

grin and bear it my mother said
it only lasts for 40 years
and then she laughed her head off

i'm sorry
we did everything we could
it's a new syndrome
before we knew what it was
it was too late

oh my god
you mean that's what caused it
i told her
never stick anything up there
now look what it's done to her

the internal protection
more women trust

3 little girls find a 10 bill
how should we spend it
i know   says the first girl
let's buy lots and lots of candy
no no   say the other two
we'd just eat it and there'd be nothing
left to show for it
i know says the second girl
let's go to a movie and buy popcorn
then we'd have entertainment and food
no no   say the other two
that's not enough   we've got to get
our money's worth
i know   says the third girl
let's buy 3 boxes of tampax
and then we can go swimming and horseback riding
and play tennis
                    and climb mountains
                              and . . .

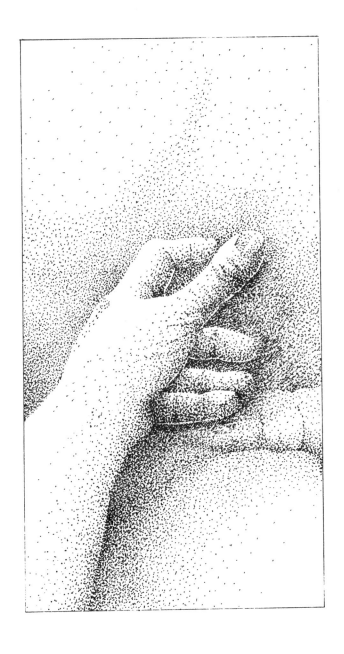

the last delivery poem

1964

it's an old-fashioned room
white tiles   black grouting
tall windows looking out on downtown toronto
a canvas curtain divides the room in two
i can see a doctor a few feet away
sitting on a stool
between a woman's legs
blood squirts out of her
she screams
he cleans his glasses

a needle in my arched spine
and i feel dizzy
then frozen from the waist down
i roll over and watch my belly heave
the nun's hand goes with it
she tells me when to push
i feel nothing

afterward
the med students and interns leave
congratulating the doctor
the nun pats my hand
you have a lovely episiotomy dear
he's so meticulous
you'd never know anything had happened
down there

1966

st. mike's again
blue room this time   windowless
filippino nurses wear flowered scrub caps
speak their own language
i have a toothache
after the spinal i roll over and start to cry
you can't feel anything can you dear says the doctor
my tooth is killing me
he orders oil of cloves which never comes

afterward
i wake up in a wet bed
red stains seep up through the bedspread
i ring for the nurse
she checks between my legs   rolls me over
blood slides off the mattress edge like jello
are you a hemophiliac says the spinal doctor
as they press bandages over the tiny hole
left in my back and tie me to a board
i lie there for two days and the bleeding stops
a dentist comes by and pulls my tooth out

1975

a stainless steel rotunda   calgary
sleepy interns talk about the grey cup
a kicking game for sure
montreal by a field goal
i watch the clock
i stop contracting   no one notices
they are waiting for the staff doctor
what are you doing travelling so close
to your due date scolds the scrub nurse
we have no charts on you
you haven't had a kid for 9 years
anything could happen
she sets up a tray near my feet

the tempo quickens when the doctor
arrives and examines me
he slaps a mask on my face
clacks a pair of forceps together
and slides them high into me
at the same moment i push my last best push
something shoots out of me
and lands in his lap
without a sound

this happened to my mother i tell anyone
they crossed her legs until the doctor came
my brother's retarded

afterward
they sew and sew   they can't stop
they run out of suture
someone brings more from another room
4th degree perineal tear says the scrub nurse
there isn't a 5th you know
this is the bloodiest delivery i ever saw
you'll be here for 2 weeks at least
the hardest part will be trying to shit

she hands me a mirror
you burst all the blood vessels in your face
with that last push
you're gonna look pretty ugly for a while

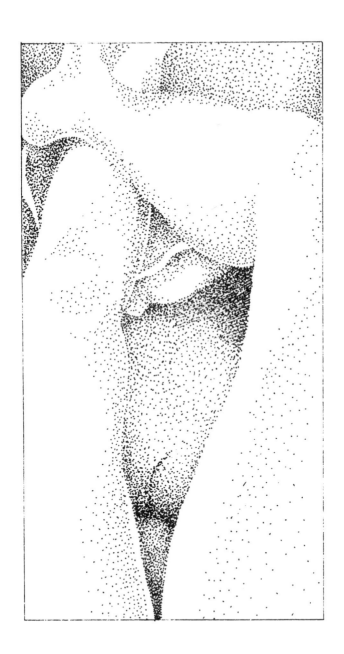

Other books available from Longspoon Press:

Raymond Gariépy, **VOICE STORM**. $7.50.

Karen Lawrence, **THE INANNA POEMS**. $7.50.

Miriam Mandel, **WHERE HAVE YOU BEEN**. $7.50.

bp nichol, **EXTREME POSITIONS**. $7.50.

Stephen Scobie, **A GRAND MEMORY FOR FORGETTING**. $8.50.

J.O. Thompson, **ECHO AND MONTANA**. $7.50.

Jon Whyte. **GALLIMAUFRY**. $9.50.

HOW TO ORDER

Longspoon Press books are not widely available in bookstores. We ask you to write directly to us:

> Longspoon Press
> c/o Dept. of English
> University of Alberta
> Edmonton, Alberta T6G 2E5

Pre-payment would be appreciated.

SPECIAL DISCOUNT PRICES

Any FOUR titles may be purchased at a discount of 30 percent.

Date Due